E

SRA **Specific Skill Series**
for Language Arts

Usage

Leveled Books
in Nine Key
Language Arts Skill Areas

SRA
Columbus, OH

The McGraw-Hill Companies

Cover: ©Tim Flach/Getty Images, Inc.

SRAonline.com

Mc Graw Hill SRA

Send all inquiries to:
SRA/McGraw-Hill
8787 Orion Place
Columbus, OH 43240-4027

Printed in the United States of America.

ISBN 0-07-601702-8

3 4 5 6 7 8 9 RHR 15 14 13 12 11 10

TO THE TEACHER

GENERAL INFORMATION ON USAGE

Usage involves the word choices people make when speaking and writing. Word choice is governed by dialect, which varies over time, across national and geographical boundaries, by gender, across age groups, and by socio-economic status. Every language has a prestige dialect associated with education and financial success. In the United States, this dialect is known as Standard English and is the language of school and business.

The study of usage helps students avoid making errors in word choice when writing—errors that can jeopardize a writer's credibility. It also helps them become confident, effective speakers.

ABOUT *SPECIFIC SKILL SERIES FOR LANGUAGE ARTS*

Specific Skill Series for Language Arts is a companion to ***Specific Skill Series,*** a supplemental reading program that has been widely recognized for its effectiveness for over thirty years. The two series are designed and organized the same. ***Specific Skill Series for Language Arts*** consists of discrete units of practice exercises that target and reinforce fundamental language-arts skills. Units in both series are presented in multiple-choice format for standardized test practice.

ABOUT *USAGE*

The scope and sequence for Books A through H of *Usage* focuses on a variety of common usage problems including subject-verb agreement, proper use of verb tenses, pronoun-antecedent agreement, and misused words. The scope and sequence for each book is located on the last page of the book. Each unit includes

- **rule boxes** that explain usage rules.
- **models** in each rule box to illustrate the language point being discussed.
- **multiple-choice exercises** for skills practice and reinforcement.

Four **Language Activity Pages** (LAPs) appear in each book. Each LAP is divided into the following four sections and reviews the skills practiced in the preceding units:

Exercising Your Skill reviews key terms and concepts.

Expanding Your Skill provides mixed practice.

Exploring Language shows how the skills apply to real-world contexts by featuring one of six forms of writing: descriptive, narrative, personal, persuasive, expository, and poetry.

Expressing Yourself includes two creative activities related to the skills. One activity is always a Work-with-a-Partner activity to encourage collaborative learning.

TO THE TEACHER

SERIES COMPONENTS

- **Student Editions:** Nine books in each level (A–H) focus on nine skill areas: *Grammar, Usage, Mechanics, Spelling, Vocabulary, Sentences, Paragraphs, Writing Process,* and *Research.*
- **Placement Test Books:** One book for each skill area includes diagnostic tests to place students in the correct level.
- **Teacher's Manual:** Primarily an answer key, the *Teacher's Manual* also includes reproducible student worksheets and further information on how to use the program, including classroom management tips.

HOW TO USE *SPECIFIC SKILL SERIES FOR LANGUAGE ARTS*

Placing Students in Levels: The scope and sequence, complexity of skills, and readability in Levels A through H correspond to Grades 1 through 8. Students may, however, be placed in any level. For example, in the second grade, a student who needs remedial work in a specific skill may be placed in Book A, an on-level student who would benefit from skills reinforcement may be placed in Book B, and an advanced student who is ready for enrichment may be placed in Book C or higher. *Placement Tests* help place students in the correct level.

Setting: This series can be used for independent study and one-on-one practice sessions, as well as in small-group and whole-class settings. It is also effective in after-school and summer-school programs.

Getting Started: Students must have notebook paper or copies of reproducible student worksheets (located in the *Teacher's Manual*) before they begin working. Remind students not to write in the books. Students may begin in any unit of any book, depending on the skill practice they need, although it is recommended that they begin with Unit 1. As they work through the units, students should record their answers on notebook paper or on the student worksheets.

Pacing: Students should be encouraged to work at their own pace, completing a few units every day or every other day.

Scoring: Teachers should score units as soon as they have been completed. Then a discussion can be held in which students justify their answer choices.

Internet Use: Some activities, especially those in *Research,* require students to use the Internet. Students' use of the Internet should be monitored closely for content appropriateness and safety.

TO THE STUDENT

Usage refers to the rules that tell you how to use words correctly in English. Understanding these rules will help you write and speak better so your ideas are clear to others.

In Book E *Usage,* you will learn about

- Subject-Verb Agreement
- Past-Tense Verbs
- Past Tense of *Be*
- Future Tense
- Perfect Tenses
- Comparing with Adjectives and Adverbs
- Participles as Adjectives
- Double Negatives
- Indefinite and Demonstrative Pronouns
- Problem Verbs
- Misused Words

After you complete this book, you will be able to use the participle forms of verbs as adjectives. Examples are boldfaced below.

Present Participle: **Cooking** methods vary from country to country.

Past Participle: **Exhausted** chefs compete in weeklong contests.

You will also learn the difference between an indefinite pronoun and a demonstrative pronoun.

Indefinite Pronoun: **Everyone** who competes is experienced.

Demonstrative Pronoun: **Those** are the recipes he used.

Another thing you will learn is how to correctly use problem verbs, such as *sit* and *set.*

Set the apple pie on the table.

Sit next to me at dinner.

By mastering the skills in this book, you will gain confidence in your writing and speaking by knowing and following the rules of usage.

Unit 1
Subject-Verb Agreement

The **present tense** of a verb shows what is happening now.

- With plural subjects and the pronouns *I, we, you,* and *they,* use the base form of a verb.

  Tests **ask** questions on a topic. I **help** my brother study for tests.

- With singular subjects and the pronouns *he, she,* and *it,* use the verb form with an *-s* or *-es* ending.

  My brother **tells** me about test topics. He **passes** his books to me.

Magnets

Which verb correctly completes each sentence?

1. Magnets _____ objects without touching them.
   (A) pulls **(B)** pull

---

2. Magnets also _____ objects without touching them.
   (A) push **(B)** pushes

---

3. They _____ iron and some other metals.
   (A) attract **(B)** attracts

---

4. Workers _____ huge magnets to move heavy scrap metal.
   (A) uses **(B)** use

---

5. A magnetic force _____ through most glass and paper.
   (A) travel **(B)** travels

---

6. It _____ paper on many boards and filing cabinets.
   (A) hold **(B)** holds

---

7. I _____ magnets on my refrigerator right now.
   (A) see **(B)** sees

---

8. Can you _____ for magnets in your home?
   (A) search **(B)** searches

Unit 1
Subject-Verb Agreement

On the Job

9. We _____ many types of homes, garages, offices, and stores.
(A) build **(B)** builds

10. We _____ different safety gear based on the jobs we do.
(A) wears **(B)** wear

11. Doug _____ briefly as each worker does his or her job.
(A) watches **(B)** watch

12. He _____ carefully for mistakes because he is our boss.
(A) checks **(B)** check

13. A boss _____ you how to correct a mistake.
(A) tell **(B)** tells

14. A mistake _____ you something new.
(A) teaches **(B)** teach

15. Hopefully it _____ you a better person and worker.
(A) make **(B)** makes

16. The workers _____ lunch together.
(A) eats **(B)** eat

17. I _____ next to Caroline at lunch.
(A) sit **(B)** sits

18. She _____ the best yogurt and fruit for lunch.
(A) mix **(B)** mixes

Unit 1
Subject-Verb Agreement

The present tense of the verb *be* is irregular. It follows different rules.

Singular:		Plural:	
	I **am**		we **are**
	you **are**		you **are**
	he/she/it **is**		they **are**

- Singular subjects (except *I* and *you*) use *is,* and plural subjects use *are.*

  The dog **is** on the porch. The birds **are** on a branch.

The present tense of the verb *have* is also irregular.

Singular:		Plural:	
	I **have**		we **have**
	you **have**		you **have**
	he/she/it **has**		they **have**

- Singular subjects (except *I* and *you*) use *has,* and plural subjects use *have.*

  The dog **has** a blue collar. The birds **have** yellow beaks.

A Busy Day

Which verb correctly completes each sentence?

19. We _____ at the store.
(A) am **(B)** are **(C)** is

20. My mom _____ many things to do today.
(A) has **(B)** have **(C)** is

21. I _____ time to go with her as she completes her tasks.
(A) am **(B)** has **(C)** have

22. I _____ glad to be with my mom.
(A) am **(B)** are **(C)** is

23. She _____ a party to host tomorrow.
(A) has **(B)** have **(C)** are

24. Guests _____ excited to visit our new home.
(A) am **(B)** are **(C)** is

Unit 1
Subject-Verb Agreement

Family Photographs

25. We _____ a family photo taken each year.
(A) are (B) has (C) have

26. I _____ a new dress to wear when our photo is taken.
(A) have (B) am (C) has

27. My dad _____ a new hat, but he will not wear it in our photo.
(A) have (B) is (C) has

28. Grandpa _____ new glasses that he really likes.
(A) is (B) has (C) have

29. My brother _____ very excited for this year's photo.
(A) is (B) am (C) are

30. He _____ grown four inches since last year's photo!
(A) is (B) have (C) has

31. My mom _____ many friends who like to receive our family photo.
(A) is (B) have (C) has

32. She _____ proud to give our photo to other people.
(A) is (B) are (C) am

33. Family photos _____ a fine way to share part of a family's history.
(A) am (B) are (C) is

34. We _____ asking more family members to be in next year's photo.
(A) am (B) are (C) is

Unit 2
Subject-Verb Agreement

A **compound subject** is made of two or more subjects that refer to the same verb. Compound subjects can be joined by *and* or *or.* The verb in the sentence should agree with the entire subject.

- Subjects joined by *and* are plural and use the plural form of the verb.
  Incorrect: **Lori and Mike** <u>walks</u> to the restaurant.
  Correct: **Lori and Mike** <u>walk</u> to the restaurant.
- Subjects joined by *or* use the verb that agrees with the closer subject.
  Incorrect: **Lori or** <u>**Mike** leave</u> the restaurant.
  Correct: **Lori or** <u>**Mike** leaves</u> the restaurant.
- The pronoun *I* should come last when it is part of a compound subject.
  My brother and I went to Massachusetts.

Games and Sports

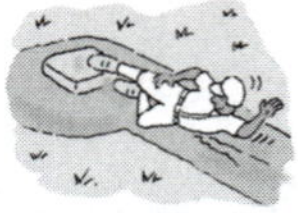

Choose the sentence from each group that is written correctly.

1. **(A)** Tennis and badminton are played with a racket.
   (B) Football and soccer is played on fields.
   (C) Surfing and snowboarding uses different types of boards.

2. **(A)** Soccer and volleyball is sports that can be played indoors.
   (B) A yellow or red card signal a foul in soccer.
   (C) Herb and I think Pelé is the greatest soccer player ever.

3. **(A)** Teams and coaches knows the rules of their sport very well.
   (B) Gloves or mitts help to protect the hands of baseball players.
   (C) Hats or helmets is worn during a baseball game.

4. **(A)** Basketball and tennis is played on courts.
   (B) Basketball and tennis have nets, but they are not the same.
   (C) Basketball or tennis are played with a ball that bounces.

5. **(A)** Basketballs and footballs feels similar.
(B) Basketballs and footballs has different shapes.
(C) Volleyballs and soccer balls are close in size.

---

6. **(A)** Simon or Kayla take karate classes.
(B) Competition and self-defense are reasons to study martial arts.
(C) Colors and degrees shows the difficulty level students have passed.

---

7. **(A)** Jeff and I know that football teams have more players off the field.
(B) Coaches and players waits in a dugout at a baseball game.
(C) Football and soccer has sidelines.

---

8. **(A)** Safety pads and helmets are very important in football.
(B) Both offense and defense works hard to win each game.
(C) Player names and numbers is on the back of football jerseys.

---

9. **(A)** Rugby or lacrosse are played on a field.
(B) Time-outs or substitutions is not allowed in rugby.
(C) Kicking, dribbling, or side passing is allowed in rugby.

---

10. **(A)** Elizabeth and I think some ancient games are like field hockey.
(B) Both field and ice hockey uses a hockey stick to hit a ball or a puck.
(C) Good eyesight and skating ability is vital to playing ice hockey well.

---

11. **(A)** Lacrosse and field hockey is not the same sport.
(B) Goals and sticks are two things these sports have in common.
(C) Ann and I sees that a lacrosse stick has a mesh or net pouch at its tip.

---

12. **(A)** Dad and I watches cricket on a new television sports channel.
(B) Dad and I learns that a batsman defends a wicket in cricket.
(C) Dad and I practice the bowling motion that cricket players use.

Unit 2
Subject-Verb Agreement

A prepositional phrase between the subject and the verb of a sentence does not change the number of the subject. Read a sentence without the phrase to decide if the subject is singular or plural.

The magazine near the sofa **is** mine. → The magazine **is** mine.

The chefs from New York **are** ready. → The chefs **are** ready.

- Some subjects that name a group use singular verbs.

This **team** of students **needs** more paint to finish the mural.

Elephants

Which verb correctly completes each sentence?

13. The class down the hall _____ about African elephants.
(A) learns **(B)** learn

14. Our class during the afternoon _____ Asian, or Indian, elephants.
(A) studies **(B)** study

15. The goal for each class _____ to collect facts on their elephant.
(A) are **(B)** is

16. Both classes meet in one room and then _____ the elephants.
(A) compares **(B)** compare

17. An audience with teachers _____ to the facts of each class.
(A) listens **(B)** listen

18. Elephants in a family unit _____ female except for male calves.
(A) is **(B)** are

19. Male calves within a family unit _____ as they grow and mature.
(A) leaves **(B)** leave

20. A family unit of grown male elephants _____ a band of bulls.
(A) is **(B)** are

Unit 2

Subject-Verb Agreement

An **inverted sentence** is a sentence where the subject comes after the verb. Inverted sentences often start with a prepositional phrase.

Between the trees **fly** many **birds**.

(**fly** = VERB; **birds** = SUBJECT)

Inverted sentences that start with *Here* or *There* follow the same rule, but they use a verb form of *be*. *Here* or *There* is never a sentence's subject.

Here **is** the **calculator**. There **are** the other **supplies**.

To see the agreement between the subject and its verb in an inverted sentence, rearrange the sentence so the subject comes before its verb.

Here **are** the **tools** you need. ⟶ The **tools** you need **are** here.

There **is** the **key** to your lock. ⟶ The **key** to your lock **is** there.

Which verb correctly completes each sentence?

21. There _____ the robe you bought.
(A) are **(B)** is

22. Here _____ the assignments you missed.
(A) are **(B)** is

23. There _____ no cabins on that mountain.
(A) are **(B)** is

24. Among the clouds _____ the sun.
(A) hide **(B)** hides

25. Here _____ the photographs I took with your camera.
(A) are **(B)** is

26. There _____ no ocean around Kentucky.
(A) are **(B)** is

27. Throughout the night _____ the frogs.
(A) sing **(B)** sings

28. Here _____ the suitcase I borrowed.
(A) are **(B)** is

Unit 3

Past-Tense Verbs

A **past-tense verb** shows action that happened already. Most verbs in the past tense are formed by adding *-d* or *-ed* to their base form.

The sailor **changed** his ship's course. Waves **splashed** upon him.

Spanish Missions in North America

Choose the correct past-tense verb to complete each sentence.

1. We _____ about Spanish missions at the museum.
   (A) learned **(B)** learn **(C)** learnd

2. The Spanish _____ in North America before the English did.
   (A) arrive **(B)** arrives **(C)** arrived

3. Francisco Coronado _____ a group toward the Southwest.
   (A) guide **(B)** guided **(C)** guides

4. Coronado and his people _____ for gold there.
   (A) searches **(B)** searched **(C)** search

5. Our speaker at the museum _____ us a map of Coronado's route.
   (A) showed **(B)** show **(C)** shows

6. The Spanish _____ the city of St. Augustine in Florida.
   (A) claims **(B)** claimed **(C)** claim

7. The Spanish _____ areas in the West also.
   (A) settle **(B)** settld **(C)** settled

8. They _____ one area Los Angeles.
   (A) names **(B)** name **(C)** named

9. People at the missions _____ orange trees and grape vines.
   (A) plant **(B)** planted **(C)** plants

10. Our speaker _____ a Spanish mission to study Spanish heritage.
    (A) visited **(B)** visit **(C)** visits

Unit 3

Past-Tense Verbs

Irregular verbs form the past tense differently. They follow one of several patterns. One pattern is when a vowel in the verb's base form changes in the past tense and in the past participle.

Base Form (happens now)	begin	sink
Past (happened already)	began	sank
Past Participle (continues from the past)	begun	sunk

Other verbs that follow this pattern include *drink, ring, shrink, sing, spring,* and *swim.*

- You will learn in a later unit that the past participle is used with the perfect tenses. Perfect tenses can show what happened in the past or what started in the past and is still happening. To use the past-participle form correctly, a form of the verb *have* must come before it.

  I **have begun** a book. He **has begun** a book. We **had begun** a book.

Choose the past verb form to correctly complete each sentence.

11. A bell _____ when it was time to get out of the pool.
(A) ring (B) rang (C) rung

12. We _____ most of the day.
(A) swam (B) swim (C) swum

13. It looked as if our fingers and toes had _____!
(A) shrink (B) shrinks (C) shrunk

14. We _____ as we walked to get our towels.
(A) sang (B) sung (C) sing

15. Then we _____ to feel hungry.
(A) begin (B) began (C) begun

16. Grumbling noises had _____ from our stomachs.
(A) springs (B) sprang (C) sprung

17. We each _____ some juice and ate a sandwich.
(A) drank (B) drink (C) drunk

18. By that time, the sun had _____ behind the trees.
(A) sink (B) sank (C) sunk

Unit 3
Past-Tense Verbs

Another irregular verb pattern is when a verb's past tense and its past participle have the same spelling. Remember that a form of the verb *have* must come before the past participle to form it correctly.

Base Form	find	lead	meet	seek
Past	found	led	met	sought
Past Participle	found	led	met	sought

Other verbs that follow this pattern include *build, buy, catch, feel, have, hold, lay, lose, make, sell, send, stand,* and *think.*

Which verb form is in the past tense?

19. We _____ land to buy in North Carolina.
(A) found **(B)** finds **(C)** find

20. We _____ a house and a garage on the land.
(A) builds **(B)** build **(C)** built

21. North Carolina has _____ its mark on the history of flight.
(A) make **(B)** made **(C)** makes

22. The Wright brothers _____ flying experiments at Kitty Hawk.
(A) held **(B)** holds **(C)** holding

23. I wonder what people in Kitty Hawk _____ of their experiments.
(A) thought **(B)** thinking **(C)** thinks

24. Wilbur and Orville Wright _____ flying success early in the 1900s.
(A) seeks **(B)** seek **(C)** sought

25. It was a trip to Kitty Hawk that _____ us to our land.
(A) led **(B)** leads **(C)** leading

26. We had _____ land before, but not with so many trees!
(A) buy **(B)** bought **(C)** buys

Unit 3

Past-Tense Verbs

More verbs that have the same past and past-participle spelling are *bring, creep, fight, get, keep, leave, lend, pay, say, sit, sleep, spend, spin, sting, swing, teach, tell,* and *win.*

Base Form	bring	keep	pay	sting
Past	brought	kept	paid	stung
Past Participle	brought	kept	paid	stung

Which verb form is in the past tense?

27. My dad had _____ me how to fix a flat tire before I could drive.
(A) teach (B) taught (C) teaching

28. My dad _____ me I could practice by changing my bicycle's tire.
(A) told (B) tell (C) tells

29. He also _____ that fixing a car tire is different than fixing a bicycle tire.
(A) saying (B) said (C) say

30. I _____ and watched as my dad showed me the process.
(A) sit (B) sits (C) sat

31. I had _____ the tools my dad needed before he started.
(A) brings (B) bring (C) brought

32. He _____ asking if I had any questions.
(A) kept (B) keeping (C) keep

33. I did not have questions because I had _____ close attention.
(A) pay (B) paid (C) pays

34. My dad went in the house and _____ his car keys.
(A) getting (B) get (C) got

35. We _____ the rest of the afternoon cruising in the car.
(A) spent (B) spends (C) spend

Unit 4

Past-Tense Verbs

There are more irregular past-tense verb patterns. Here are three verbs with the same base and past-participle forms, but a different past form.

Base Form (happens now)	become	come	run
Past (happened already)	became	came	ran
Past Participle (continues from past)	become	come	run

The following verbs have the same base, past, and past-participle forms: *burst, cost, cut, hit, hurt, let, put, read, set,* and *spread.* Remember, to use a past participle correctly, a form of the verb *have* comes before it.

She **put** her car in their garage. He **had** **put** his car away already.

Civilizations

Which past-tense verb form correctly completes each sentence?

1. The Maya _____ through many places we know of today.
   (A) spread **(B)** spreaded

2. Parts of Mexico, Belize, and Honduras _____ home to the Maya.
   (A) became **(B)** become

3. I had _____ that they dwelled in areas of Guatemala and El Salvador.
   (A) readed **(B)** read

4. The Indus Valley people had _____ up their towns in what is now Iran.
   (A) set **(B)** setted

5. Roads in these ancient towns _____ straight, similar to streets today.
   (A) run **(B)** ran

6. Marco Polo had _____ from Persia to China along the Silk Road.
   (A) came **(B)** come

7. He _____ others know about China before any other European.
   (A) letted **(B)** let

8. By the 1400s, Asia's wonderful goods had _____ European markets.
   (A) hit **(B)** hitted

Unit 4

Past-Tense Verbs

Irregular verbs can also have exceptions. The following verbs in their past-tense and past-participle forms do *not* follow a pattern: *be, do, go, lie, tear,* and *wear.* These verbs still use a form of the verb *have* to form their past participles, such as *has torn* and *had worn.*

Base Form	be	do	go	lie
Past	was, were	did	went	lay
Past Participle	been	done	gone	lain

Verbs that end in *-ew* in the past-tense and *-wn* in the past-participle form include *blow, draw, fly, grow, know,* and *throw.*

Base Form	draw	fly	grow	know
Past	drew	flew	grew	knew
Past Participle	drawn	flown	grown	known

Which past-tense verb form correctly completes each sentence?

9. Prices increased many times as demand _____ on the Silk Road.
(A) grown **(B)** grew

10. Europeans had _____ looking for a cheaper way to get spices.
(A) been **(B)** were

11. In the 1400s, the Portuguese _____ they had a faster and safer ship.
(A) knew **(B)** known

12. Christopher Columbus _____ to the Americas by mistake in 1492.
(A) went **(B)** gone

13. He had _____ to Spain seventy-one days earlier.
(A) went **(B)** gone

14. Columbus _____ what he could to find a faster water route to Asia.
(A) did **(B)** done

15. Ptolemy had _____ the map Columbus used on his sailing voyage.
(A) drew **(B)** drawn

16. The map Ptolemy _____ was from the second century.
(A) drew **(B)** drawn

Unit 4

Past-Tense Verbs

Another irregular verb pattern occurs when a verb's past-participle form ends with *-en.* A form of *have* still comes before the past participle.

Base Form	break	choose	ride	take
Past	broke	chose	rode	took
Past Participle	broken	chosen	ridden	taken

Other verbs that follow this pattern are *drive, freeze, shake,* and *steal.*

Which past-tense verb form correctly completes each sentence?

17. Our family _____ to stay in the house because of the snowstorm.
(A) chose **(B)** chosen

18. My parents had _____ in storms, so they knew we were safer indoors.
(A) drove **(B)** driven

19. The forceful winds _____ the windows of our home.
(A) shaken **(B)** shook

20. We sat away from the windows in case any _____ or shattered.
(A) broken **(B)** broke

21. Ice had _____ onto parts of our house.
(A) frozen **(B)** froze

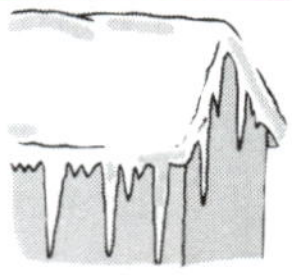

22. Some of us _____ sleds outside to play in the snow.
(A) taken **(B)** took

23. I _____ a garbage bag from our garage to slide on in the snow.
(A) stole **(B)** stolen

24. It was so cold that none of us _____ sleds or played in the snow.
(A) rode **(B)** ridden

25. Once we had _____ to go inside, we were excited for warm soup.
(A) chose **(B)** chosen

Unit 4

Past-Tense Verbs

More verbs that end with *-en* in the past-participle form include *bite, eat, fall, give, rise, see, speak,* and *write.*

Base Form	eat	fall	give	speak
Past	ate	fell	gave	spoke
Past Participle	eaten	fallen	given	spoken

Which past-tense verb form correctly completes each sentence?

26. My brother _____ and sent me a letter from college.
(A) wrote **(B)** written

27. He had _____ a guest speaker who talked about stars and planets.
(A) saw **(B)** seen

28. My brother remembered that I had _____ about such things before.
(A) spoken **(B)** spoke

29. I _____ from my chair when I noticed something on the floor.
(A) risen **(B)** rose

30. The speaker had _____ his listeners a postcard with a planet on it.
(A) given **(B)** gave

31. The postcard _____ out of the envelope when I opened my letter.
(A) fallen **(B)** fell

32. My brother had _____ to ask me to name which planet it was.
(A) wrote **(B)** written

33. I _____ the postcard and knew right away that the planet was Mars.
(A) saw **(B)** seen

34. I _____ into my lunch only once as I started a letter to my brother.
(A) bit **(B)** bitten

35. I had _____ as much as I could before I decided to call him instead.
(A) ate **(B)** eaten

Unit 5

Past Tense of *Be*

The past tense of the verb *be* is irregular. It follows different rules.

Singular:		Plural:	
	I **was**		we **were**
	you **were**		you **were**
	he/she/it **was**		they **were**

Singular subjects (except for *you*) use *was,* and plural subjects use *were.*

The library **was** closed. The restaurants **were** closed.

- The past tense of *be* also comes before a verb that ends with *-ing.* When an action continues from the past, use the following forms of *be.*

Singular:		Plural:	
	I **was** looking.		We **were** looking.
	You **were** looking.		You **were** looking.
	He/She/It **was** looking.		They **were** looking.

Which verb form correctly completes each sentence?

1. Librarians _____ a large pile of books by subject.
   (A) was classifying **(B)** were classifying

2. They _____ book titles and summaries.
   (A) was reading **(B)** were reading

3. Numbers on the books _____ a certain pattern.
   (A) were following **(B)** was following

4. One librarian _____ a list of the book numbers.
   (A) were typing **(B)** was typing

5. Another librarian _____ book authors on a new spreadsheet.
   (A) was tracking **(B)** were tracking

6. Spreadsheets _____ records of the books each librarian found.
   (A) were keeping **(B)** was keeping

7. A different librarian _____ the spreadsheets on a computer.
   (A) was maintaining **(B)** were maintaining

Unit 5

Past Tense of *Be*

Our School Swim Meet

8. People from our town _____ an important swimming event.
(A) was watching **(B)** were watching

9. They _____ at a pool that is close to where my family and I live.
(A) were **(B)** was

10. The swim meet _____ outside because of the pleasant weather.
(A) was **(B)** were

11. I _____ at the swim meet to watch my friend Stella compete.
(A) were **(B)** was

12. My dad _____ with me until he decided to cook a special dinner.
(A) was going **(B)** were going

13. My sister _____, but she took a break to spend time with me.
(A) were studying **(B)** was studying

14. Stella _____ when my sister and I found her.
(A) were stretching **(B)** was stretching

15. We _____ where we could see the pool well.
(A) was standing **(B)** were standing

16. Stella's brother _____ in a race at that time.
(A) was swimming **(B)** were swimming

17. We _____ very happy when he won the race.
(A) was **(B)** were

18. I _____ nervous for Stella's race to begin.
(A) was **(B)** were

The First LAP
Language Activity Pages

A. Exercising Your Skill

You have been learning about compound subjects, inverted sentences, verbs in the present, past, and past-participle forms, and irregular verbs. Number your paper from 1 to 8. Read the sentences below. Use a word from the box only once to complete each sentence correctly.

present	Singular	irregular	Plural
inverted	two	past	prepositional

1. The _____ tense of a verb shows what is happening now.
2. The _____ tense of a verb shows what happened already.
3. Verbs that are _____ follow different rules for forming tenses.
4. The subject comes after the verb in an _____ sentence.
5. A compound subject has _____ or more subjects for the same verb.
6. When a _____ phrase is used between the subject and the verb of a sentence, the number of the subject does not change.
7. _____ subjects refer to one.
8. _____ subjects refer to more than one.

B. Expanding Your Skill

Number your paper from 1 to 8. Read the sentences below. Write the prepositional phrase from each sentence on your paper. If the subject of the sentence is singular, write the letter **S** on your paper. If the subject of the sentence is plural, write the letter **P** on your paper.

1. The field trip for my class is tomorrow.
2. Students in my class are very excited.
3. The zoo near the city is where we are going.
4. Animals of the zoo are guarded day and night.
5. Zoo animals throughout the day are cleaned and fed.
6. They, like people, work, play, and sleep.
7. Our trip with the zoo guides is going to teach us a lot.
8. The guides during lunch are ready to answer our questions.

C. Exploring Language

Personal Writing Number your paper from 1 to 10. Read the journal entry below. Each sentence has two verb forms, but only one is correct. Choose and write the correct verb for each sentence on your paper.

April 9, 2005

I gone/went to a play with Aunt Margo and Uncle Tim. They was/were visiting from North Dakota. They had bought/boughten the play's tickets for my birthday. We chose/chosen to see a play during the afternoon. This way the whole family eaten/ate dinner together. We met/metted at my favorite restaurant. We taken/took my best friend too. We had began/begun to order when people started to sing. They sang/sung "Happy Birthday" to me. I was/were laughing a lot!

D. Expressing Yourself

Choose one of these activities. When you are finished, give your paper to your teacher.

1. Find a newspaper or magazine article that is one to five paragraphs in length. Search for the verb *have* in any of the forms you have learned, which are *have, has,* and *had.* Remember to look for the past-participle form because the verb *have* comes before a past participle when used and written correctly. Count how many times each form of *have* is used, and write the results on your paper. Then write one sentence of your own correctly using each form of *have* that you found in the article.

2. **WORK with a PARTNER** Find a newspaper or magazine article that is two to six paragraphs in length. Work with a partner to search for the verb *be* in any of the forms you have learned, such as *am, are, was,* and *were.* Remember to look for forms of *be* that are used before other verbs that end with *-ing,* such as *were running.* List each form of *be* that you found once on your paper, and write the number of times each is used. Then write one sentence with your partner, correctly using each form of *be* that you found in the article.

Unit 6

Future Tense

The **future tense** of a verb expresses action that will take place. It is formed using the helping verb *will* before the base form of the verb.

The alarm **will ring** for the fire drill. Teachers **will lead** the drill.

In some formal situations, the helping verb *shall* is used before the base form of the verb when the subject is *I* or *we.*

I **shall consult** my client. We **shall abide** by the court's ruling.

Choose the correct future-tense form to complete each sentence.

1. We _____ in our class with gymnastic judges tomorrow morning.
   (A) shall being **(B)** shall am **(C)** shall be

2. Shelby _____ the balance beam.
   (A) will practices
   (B) will practicing
   (C) will practice

3. The balance beam _____ to be safe and secure.
   (A) will needs **(B)** will need **(C)** will needing

4. The coaches _____ all of the equipment carefully.
   (A) will check **(B)** will checks **(C)** will checking

5. I _____ the pommel horse, which is a short, thick beam with handles.
   (A) will learning **(B)** will learns **(C)** will learn

6. The pommel horse _____ my gymnastic skill.
   (A) will challenge **(B)** will challenging **(C)** will challenges

7. I _____ the judges evaluate my performance.
   (A) shall having **(B)** shall has **(C)** shall have

8. The class _____ at noon.
   (A) will ends **(B)** will ending **(C)** will end

Unit 6
Future Tense

Verbs can tell about an action that begins and continues in the future.

- Use *will be* before a verb that ends with *-ing*.

  Matt **will be attending** college.

  Students **will be attending** college.

- With the pronouns *I* and *we*, *shall be* can be used before *-ing* verbs.

  I shall be dining when you call.

  We **shall be dining** when you call.

Monday at the Museum

Which verb form correctly completes each sentence?

9. My mom _____ home from work by 3:00 P.M.
(A) will arrives (B) will arrive (C) will arriving

10. My dad _____ home around 4:00 P.M.
(A) will come (B) will coming (C) will comes

11. We _____ to the History Museum after dinner.
(A) shall be go (B) shall going (C) shall be going

12. For dinner, we _____ salad and pasta at home.
(A) shall eating (B) shall eat (C) shall eats

13. The museum _____ drawings by North American architects.
(A) will displays (B) will displaying (C) will be displaying

14. I _____ about being an architect when I see the drawings.
(A) shall be thinking (B) shall be think (C) shall thinking

15. The museum _____ a brief film about architecture also.
(A) will be shows (B) will showing (C) will be showing

16. My parents and I _____ the film at 7:15 P.M.
(A) will viewing (B) will be viewing (C) will be view

Unit 7
Perfect Tenses

Use the **present-perfect tense** of a verb to tell about an action that happened at some time in the past and may still be happening. To form this tense, use *has* or *have* before the verb's past participle.

Aimee **has sent** the invitations. We **have received** ours.

Choose the present-perfect tense to correctly complete each sentence.

1. Manuel _____ to build a birdhouse.
   (A) have started **(B)** has starting **(C)** has started

2. Friends _____ parts of the birdhouse for Manuel.
   (A) have painted **(B)** have paint **(C)** has painted

3. They _____ Manuel, so some birds will have a home sooner.
   (A) have helped **(B)** has helped **(C)** have helping

4. One bird family _____ outside of Manuel's attic for many years.
   (A) has nesting **(B)** has nested **(C)** has nest

5. Manuel _____ his birdhouse with the hope that the bird family will live in it.
   (A) have designed **(B)** has designing **(C)** has designed

6. Manuel _____ a special type of glue for his birdhouse.
   (A) has purchases **(B)** has purchased **(C)** have purchased

7. The glue _____ as safe for animals and the environment.
   (A) has tested **(B)** have tested **(C)** has testing

8. The paint products Manuel will use _____ safety requirements too.
   (A) have metted **(B)** have meet **(C)** have met

9. The birdhouses in Manuel's yard _____ many baby birds through the years.
   (A) has protected **(B)** have protected **(C)** have protects

Unit 7

Perfect Tenses

Use the **past-perfect tense** of a verb to tell about an action that happened before another action or event in the past. To form this tense, use *had* before the verb's past participle.

Judd **had mailed** an anniversary card to his parents. His parents **had opened** it.

The past-perfect tense is often used in a sentence when a past-tense verb occurs in another part of the sentence.

He **had planned** on giving it to them before he <u>left</u> on his business trip.

Choose the past-perfect tense to correctly complete each sentence.

10. Manuel ______ the birdhouse by the time spring arrived.
(A) had finished (B) had finish (C) had finishing

11. Manuel ______ a list of new project ideas in a notebook.
(A) had writes (B) had written (C) had wrote

12. Before long, Manuel ______ on his next project.
(A) had decided (B) had decides (C) had deciding

13. After Manuel ______ his sister's birthday wish, he knew what to do.
(A) had hearing (B) had hear (C) had heard

14. His sister ______ for a bulletin board to display cards, photos, and art.
(A) had asked (B) had asking (C) had asks

15. Manuel ______ that his sister would want a dollhouse, which was more difficult to build.
(A) had thinking (B) had think (C) had thought

16. In the past, Manuel ______ a simple dollhouse for his cousin's birthday in May.
(A) had completes (B) had complete (C) had completed

17. By the end of the week, he ______ all of the supplies he needed for his sister's bulletin board.
(A) had purchasing (B) had purchased (C) had purchase

Unit 7

Perfect Tenses

Use the **future-perfect tense** of a verb to tell about an action that will be completed before another action or event in the future. To form this tense, use *will have* or *shall have* before the verb's past participle.

When I finish this book, I **will have read** three books this week.

Remember to use the correct tense to express the time of an action.

Present-Perfect Tense: Walter **has called** his boss.

Past-Perfect Tense: Walter **had thought** he was ill, so he made a doctor's appointment.

Future-Perfect Tense: Walter **will have missed** only two days of work if he comes back tomorrow.

Choose the correct tense from the box to complete each sentence.

(A) had built	**(B)** will have helped	**(C)** has worked

18. **Present-Perfect Tense:** Manuel _____ on several projects.

19. **Past-Perfect Tense:** By the time he was ten years old he _____ a table and four chairs.

20. **Future-Perfect Tense:** Manuel's dad _____ him with several projects by the end of the year.

(A) has created	**(B)** had asked	**(C)** will have been

21. **Present-Perfect Tense:** Manuel _____ some pieces of furniture to give as gifts.

22. **Past-Perfect Tense:** Keira, Manuel's sister, _____ Manuel to design a bulletin board for her.

23. **Future-Perfect Tense:** The bulletin board _____ on her wall for two years when she turns thirteen next week.

(A) has used	**(B)** had taught	**(C)** will have handled

24. **Present-Perfect Tense:** Manuel's dad _____ a lot of power tools.

25. **Past-Perfect Tense:** He _____ Manuel to work safely with tools before Manuel even learned to ride a bike.

26. **Future-Perfect Tense:** Manuel _____ a hammer hundreds of times by now.

Unit 7
Perfect Tenses

(A) has reduced	(B) will have spent	(C) had believed

27. Present-Perfect Tense: Using tools _____ the amount of time Manuel spends on projects.

28. Past-Perfect Tense: Manuel _____ that he wanted to be an electrician.

29. Future-Perfect Tense: If Manuel buys the new tools he needs, he _____ all of his allowance money.

(A) had selected	(B) will have rented	(C) has read

30. Present-Perfect Tense: Manuel _____ many books on woodworking.

31. Past-Perfect Tense: He _____ videos at the library about making furniture.

32. Future-Perfect Tense: He _____ all of the videos at least twice before he begins his next big project.

(A) has turned	(B) had found	(C) will have turned

33. Present-Perfect Tense: Manuel _____ some trash into treasure.

34. Past-Perfect Tense: He _____ a shelf and a chair no one else wanted and turned them into usable furniture.

35. Future-Perfect Tense: He _____ both pieces into usable furniture.

(A) had learned	(B) have made	(C) will have developed

36. Present-Perfect Tense: Effort and patience _____ Manuel successful.

37. Past-Perfect Tense: Manuel _____ quickly what he loved to do.

38. Future-Perfect Tense: By the time he is an adult, it is likely that his hobby _____ into a career.

Unit 8

Comparing with Adjectives and Adverbs

Comparisons in writing can provide readers with a clearer picture. **Adjectives,** or words that describe nouns and pronouns, help to compare nouns. They can show the level of a comparison.

Nuts are a **good** snack.	Mud smells **bad**.
Fruit is a **better** snack than nuts.	Glue smells **worse** than mud.
Cereal is the **best** snack of all.	Tar smells the **worst** of all three.

- An adjective's **comparative** form compares one person or thing with another and usually ends with *-er,* such as *My soil is **richer** than his soil.*
- An adjective's **superlative** form compares one person or thing with several others and usually ends with *-est,* such as *Your soil is the **richest** in the neighborhood.*

Which adjective correctly completes each sentence?

1. That is a _____ light than the kitchen light.
   (A) brightest **(B)** brighter

2. I work in a building _____ than your building.
   (A) tallest **(B)** taller

3. Which tree is the _____ of all the trees in the park?
   (A) oldest **(B)** older

4. Of all known cave systems, Mammoth Cave National Park is the _____.
   (A) larger **(B)** largest

5. The music from the concert was _____ than my car's radio.
   (A) louder **(B)** loudest

6. Hawaii might be the _____ place in the world to surf.
   (A) best **(B)** better

7. The store's manager was _____ than the store's cashier.
   (A) friendlier **(B)** friendliest

8. This is the _____ article I have ever read in a newspaper.
   (A) worse **(B)** worst

Unit 8
Comparing with Adjectives and Adverbs

Use these adjectives to compare the amount, or how many, of something: *many, more, most, little, less,* and *least.*

Leo has **many** books.
She has **more** books than Leo.
I have the **most** books of all of us.

We own **little** land.
They own **less** land than we.
You own the **least** land of all.

Which adjective correctly completes each sentence?

9. Out of all the campers, Karl showed the ____ attention to the noise.
(A) least **(B)** little

10. These shoes are ____ expensive than those shoes.
(A) little **(B)** less

11. California has ____ people than Vermont.
(A) more **(B)** many

12. Which insect has the ____ legs?
(A) most **(B)** more

13. She has ____ to paint than I do.
(A) least **(B)** less

14. The ____ attention was paid to my speech out of all the candidates.
(A) less **(B)** least

15. Does Denmark have ____ snow than Norway?
(A) more **(B)** most

16. Do you know which English word has the ____ letters?
(A) many **(B)** most

17. I think ____ cars are on the road than motorcycles.
(A) more **(B)** most

18. The wall map is ____ confusing than this map.
(A) less **(B)** least

Unit 8

Comparing with Adjectives and Adverbs

Adverbs, or words that modify verbs, adjectives, or other adverbs, help to compare actions. They can show the level of a comparison.

He rows **slowly**. She rows **slower** than he does. I row **slowest** of all.

- An adverb's **comparative** form compares one action with another and usually ends with *-er.*

  Mei arrived **later** than Frank did.

- An adverb's **superlative** form compares one action with several others and usually ends with *-est.*

  Ida arrived **latest** to class.

- Some irregular adverbs include *well, better, best; badly, worse, worst; little, less, least; far, farther, farthest;* and *far, further, furthest.*

  far/farther/farthest show distance: Today you rowed the **farthest**.

  far/further/furthest show degree: I do not know anything **further**.

Which adverb correctly completes each sentence?

19. On our track team, you run the _____.
(A) quicker (B) quickest

20. I know _____ about this topic than Justin does.
(A) less (B) least

21. Melanie sings _____ than her sister.
(A) worst (B) worse

22. Which of the seven cars does Eric like _____?
(A) well (B) best

23. The mayor cannot speak _____ on this issue.
(A) further (B) furthest

24. The Smiths arrived _____ of all the guests.
(A) earliest (B) earlier

25. We hiked _____ up the path than the other group.
(A) farther (B) farthest

Unit 8
Comparing with Adjectives and Adverbs

Which adjective or adverb correctly completes each sentence?

26. Their guests drove _____ than our guests.
(A) farther (B) farthest

27. The river by the cabin floods the _____ of all.
(A) worse (B) worst

28. In all of the state, the _____ college is downtown.
(A) best (B) better

29. Wearing these shoes, I ran _____ than you did.
(A) worse (B) badly

30. Louise has _____ hats than Bonnie.
(A) most (B) more

31. Dusting is what Henry enjoys the _____ of all his chores.
(A) least (B) less

32. The bird was _____ than the cat.
(A) quietest (B) quieter

33. I study _____ in a quiet place than a noisy place.
(A) better (B) well

34. Which town has the _____ swimming pools in all the county?
(A) bad (B) worst

35. Patrick plays his saxophone _____ than his clarinet.
(A) loudly (B) louder

36. We eat _____ soup in the summer than the winter.
(A) less (B) least

Unit 9
Participles as Adjectives

The participle forms of a verb can act as adjectives to describe nouns.

- The present participle uses the *-ing* form of the verb.
  The game ended with a **shocking** score.
- The past participle ends in *-d,* or *-ed* or uses an irregular form.
  Tired teams walked off the field. **Thrilled** fans cheered!
  Fallen signs were collected by remaining spectators.

A Backyard Brunch

Choose the word to correctly complete each sentence.

1. Working as a chef is my mom's _____ career.
   (A) chosed **(B)** chosen

2. It was not a _____ choice for her.
   (A) surprising **(B)** surprise

3. My mom enjoys _____ experiments.
   (A) cook **(B)** cooking

4. On Saturday, a _____ brunch was held in our backyard.
   (A) planned **(B)** plan

5. _____ invitations were mailed to my mom's guests.
   (A) Completed **(B)** Completes

6. _____ food was not used during my mom's preparation.
   (A) Frozed **(B)** Frozen

7. In fact, she used many _____ foods.
   (A) imported **(B)** import

8. Guests feasted on tasty main dishes and _____ desserts.
   (A) appeal **(B)** appealing

9. _____ guests departed with leftovers and a smile.
   (A) Impress **(B)** Impressed

Unit 9
Participles as Adjectives

What's in the News?

10. _____ stories in a newspaper are called *articles.*
(A) Writed **(B)** Written

11. Long hours and _____ research go into many articles.
(A) tiring **(B)** tire

12. A newspaper's _____ events include art, sports, politics, and finance.
(A) covered **(B)** covers

13. _____ editors can improve a reporter's article.
(A) Skill **(B)** Skilled

14. Letters to the editor are sent to the newspaper by _____ readers.
(A) willing **(B)** will

15. The _____ section lists jobs, homes, apartments, sales, and services.
(A) classify **(B)** classified

16. _____ items, such as cars, boats, and furniture, are also listed.
(A) Use **(B)** Used

17. Details about _____ property may be in a newspaper.
(A) stoled **(B)** stolen

18. _____ ideas can be found in several newspapers.
(A) Landscaping **(B)** Landscapes

19. Weather forecasts and _____ recipes are in newspapers.
(A) bake **(B)** baking

20. _____ authors sometimes contribute articles to a newspaper.
(A) Known **(B)** Knowed

The Second LAP
Language Activity Pages

A. Exercising Your Skill

You have been learning how to form the future and perfect tenses of verbs, how to compare with adjectives and adverbs, and how to use a verb's present- or past- participle form as an adjective. Number your paper from 1 to 6. Read the sentences below. Use a word from the box only once to complete each sentence correctly.

superlative	participle	past	present	future	comparative

1. The _____-perfect tense expresses action that happened already, but when it happened is unclear.
2. The _____-perfect tense expresses action that happened before another action or event.
3. The _____-perfect tense expresses action that will be completed before another action or event.
4. The _____ form compares one action, person, or thing with another.
5. The _____ form compares one action, person, or thing with several others.
6. The _____ forms of a verb can act as adjectives to describe nouns.

B. Expanding Your Skill

Number your paper from 1 to 8. Read the sentences below. For each underlined verb form, write *present* if the tense is present perfect, write *past* if it is past perfect, and write *future* if it is future perfect.

1. I have seen that movie.
2. My friends had told me it was worth seeing.
3. That actress has starred in other movies.
4. By the end of the year, she will have appeared in four feature films.
5. Have you read any reviews of her latest film?
6. Had she acted in any comedies before this one?
7. Critics have called her "the next Audrey Hepburn."
8. I am sure I will have seen her in many more movies by this time next year.

C. Exploring Language

Descriptive Writing Number your paper from 1 to 7. Read the paragraph below. Write each comparative adjective or adverb and each superlative adjective or adverb that you find.

My family and I moved to another neighborhood. Our new house is smaller than our previous house. There were more rooms in our old house than in our new one, but we did not use all of them. It was the best time to move because the school year had not started yet. Though we live farther away from my school than before, there is less traffic, and I get to ride a bus. My new room is the nicest I have ever had. I have a window that is bigger than my bed! I can watch birds from my window. I am excited to live in a different place.

D. Expressing Yourself

Choose one of these activities. When you are finished, give your paper to your teacher.

1. Think of an event that you are looking forward to, such as a sports game, a concert, a vacation, or a field trip. Write a list of words to describe how you think the event will make you feel and how the actual event will be. Write a short paragraph about the event you are looking forward to. Use some of the words from your list in the paragraph. Since the event is in the future, be sure to use the future tense.

2. **WORK with a PARTNER** Look around your classroom for verbs. With a partner, write a list of ten verbs. Below your list or on the back of the same paper, make three columns. Write the title *Present-Perfect Tense* at the top of the first column. Write *Past-Perfect Tense* at the top of the second column. Finally, write *Future-Perfect Tense* at the top of the last column. Based on what you have learned about perfect tenses, write the three forms for each of the verbs on your list. For example, look at the verb *read*: *has read* or *have read, had read, will have read* or *shall have read.* Remember, some verbs have irregular forms.

Unit 10

Double Negatives

Not is a **negative word** that expresses the idea of "no." Remember that *n't* in a contraction stands for *not.* Negative words have opposites known as **affirmative words,** or words that express the idea of "yes."

Negative	**Affirmative**
never, scarcely, hardly, barely	always, ever
nobody	anybody, everybody, somebody
no, none	all, any, one, some
no one	anyone, everyone, one, someone
nothing	anything, something
nowhere	anywhere, somewhere

- Using two negative words to express the same idea is called a **double negative,** such as *I don't have* ***no*** *dimes* or *I do* ***not*** *have* ***no*** *dimes.* Only one negative word is needed to express the same idea. One way to correct a double negative is to remove one of the negative words.

  I do**n't** have **no** dimes. ⟶ I have **no** dimes.

  Or, replace one of the negative words with an affirmative word.

  I do**n't** have **no** dimes. ⟶ I don't have **any** dimes.

Which sentence does *not* have a double negative?

1. **(A)** The payment didn't barely cover her expenses.
   (B) The payment didn't cover no expenses.
   (C) The payment barely covered her expenses.

2. **(A)** The squirrels did not have no food to survive.
   (B) The squirrels did not have scarcely any food to survive.
   (C) The squirrels had scarcely enough food to survive.

3. **(A)** There is no need to be afraid of the thunder.
   (B) There isn't no need to be afraid of the thunder.
   (C) There isn't never need to be afraid of the thunder.

4. **(A)** At first we couldn't see nothing.
   (B) At first we couldn't see anything.
   (C) At first we couldn't see no one.

5. **(A)** We looked for a store, but there were not any open.
(B) We looked for a store, but there were not none open.
(C) We looked for a store, but there were not nothing open.

6. **(A)** I can barely believe the story about the storm.
(B) I can't barely believe the story about the storm.
(C) I can barely believe no story about the storm.

7. **(A)** When we won, we could not scarcely control our excitement.
(B) When we won, we could not control no excitement.
(C) When we won, we could scarcely control our excitement.

8. **(A)** We don't know nothing about the theft.
(B) We don't know anything about the theft.
(C) We don't know anything about no theft.

9. **(A)** He was not never taller than his father.
(B) He was not no taller than his father.
(C) He was not any taller than his father.

10. **(A)** The farmer does not go anywhere during harvest time.
(B) The farmer never goes nowhere during harvest time.
(C) The farmer does not go nowhere during harvest time.

11. **(A)** The sailors don't have scarcely any more supplies.
(B) The sailors don't have no more supplies.
(C) The sailors don't have any more supplies.

12. **(A)** These shorts don't hardly fit me anymore.
(B) These shorts hardly fit me anymore.
(C) These shorts hardly fit me no more.

Unit 11
Indefinite Pronouns

An **indefinite pronoun** is used to refer to a person, a place, or a thing that is not specific. The following indefinite pronouns are always singular and use a singular verb: *another, anybody, anyone, anything, each, either, everybody, everyone, everything, much, neither, nobody, nothing, no one, one, somebody, someone,* and *something.*

- When *another, each, either, neither, one,* or *much* is used as a subject, a phrase that appears between the subject and the verb does not change the fact that the verb is singular.

    Each of the phones **is** ringing. ⟶ **Each is** ringing.
    Each of the phones **rings** loudly. ⟶ **Each rings** loudly.

Which verb correctly completes each sentence?

1. This restroom facility closes at 7:00 P.M.; another near the lake ____ at 8:00 P.M.
   (A) close **(B)** closes

2. Everybody throughout the building ____ the owner.
   (A) greets **(B)** greet

3. No one ____ on Monday night.
   (A) perform **(B)** performs

4. Either ____ too far away from here to walk.
   (A) are **(B)** is

5. Anyone from our school ____ the answer.
   (A) knows **(B)** know

6. Something inside the box ____ onto the floor.
   (A) drip **(B)** drips

7. Much ____ at risk during a severe storm.
   (A) is **(B)** are

8. Anything above that shelf ____ for a reduced price.
   (A) sells **(B)** sell

Unit 11

Indefinite Pronouns

These indefinite pronouns are always plural and use a plural verb: *both, few, many, others,* and *several.* Phrases that are used between the subject and the verb do *not* change that the subject is plural.

Few on the team **are** absent. ⟶ **Few are** absent.

Few across the field **clap** for us. ⟶ **Few clap** for us.

Which verb correctly completes each sentence?

9. Many of the animals _____ in a type of group.
   (A) live **(B)** lives

10. Few aboard the ship _____ the sunrise.
    (A) watches **(B)** watch

11. Both with much skill _____ the race.
    (A) finish **(B)** finishes

12. Others _____ silver or gold trim.
    (A) has **(B)** have

13. Several _____ at the theater to learn about acting.
    (A) work **(B)** works

14. Few during the day _____ out to fly.
    (A) comes **(B)** come

15. Many _____ the same question when they visit the museum.
    (A) asks **(B)** ask

16. Several _____ well of your talent.
    (A) speak **(B)** speaks

17. Others around the area _____ just as happy with the results.
    (A) is **(B)** are

18. Both _____ to a town out west.
    (A) relocate **(B)** relocates

Unit 11
Indefinite Pronouns

The following indefinite pronouns can be singular or plural: *all, any, most, none,* and *some.* If a phrase follows one of these pronouns, use the phrase's last word to decide if the pronoun is singular or plural.

Singular: **All** of the milk **tastes** good. **Most** of the milk **is** cold.

Plural: **All** of the grades **pass**. **Most** of the grades **are** correct.

Which verb correctly completes each sentence?

19. All of the farmer's pumpkins _____ plump and orange.
(A) are **(B)** is

20. None of the students _____ to read the assignment.
(A) volunteers **(B)** volunteer

21. Most of the yard's grass _____ better with less water.
(A) grows **(B)** grow

22. Any of our vehicles _____ all right for such a short journey.
(A) are **(B)** is

23. Some of the jurors _____.
(A) agree **(B)** agrees

24. None of the snow _____ plowed.
(A) are **(B)** is

25. All of these roads _____ speed bumps.
(A) have **(B)** has

26. Some of the lakes _____ at this point.
(A) meets **(B)** meet

27. Any of your paintings _____ on that wall.
(A) fits **(B)** fit

28. Most of his research _____ awards.
(A) receives **(B)** receive

Unit 11
Indefinite Pronouns

Most indefinite pronouns are always singular, such as *one,* and use singular verbs. Others are always plural, such as *few,* and use plural verbs. Some indefinite pronouns are singular or plural, such as *some.* When a phrase appears between an indefinite pronoun and its verb, use the last word of the phrase to decide which verb form to use.

Which verb correctly completes each sentence?

29. Everything beside the curb _____ for charity.
(A) are **(B)** is

30. Several _____ to win the prize.
(A) hope **(B)** hopes

31. Neither _____ without the proper shoes.
(A) jog **(B)** jogs

32. Anybody except your parents _____ your performance.
(A) judge **(B)** judges

33. Others _____ to Central America.
(A) travel **(B)** travels

34. Most of the hotel rooms _____ reserved.
(A) are **(B)** is

35. Each _____ to the dry cleaner.
(A) go **(B)** goes

36. Many beyond her house _____ the sidewalk.
(A) shade **(B)** shades

37. Someone since yesterday _____ bought the dress.
(A) have **(B)** has

38. Nothing _____ on tomorrow's agenda.
(A) is **(B)** are

Unit 12

Demonstrative Pronouns

A **demonstrative pronoun** refers to a specific person, place, or thing.

- *This* is singular, and *these* is plural. Both pronouns refer to things that are nearby.

  This is a long road. **These are** helpful maps.

- *That* is singular, and *those* is plural. Both pronouns refer to things that are at a distance.

  That is my brother's house. **Those were** the trees we planted.

Which pronoun correctly completes each sentence?

1. _____ washes out a juice stain.
   (A) This **(B)** These

2. Kelly thinks _____ is a smart idea.
   (A) that **(B)** those

3. _____ are the wrong directions.
   (A) These **(B)** This

4. _____ moves us to third place.
   (A) These **(B)** This

5. _____ take too long to bake.
   (A) Those **(B)** That

6. Cameron knows _____ makes us late.
   (A) these **(B)** this

7. _____ is not your guitar.
   (A) Those **(B)** That

8. _____ stay on the porch.
   (A) These **(B)** This

9. My grandparents said _____ have seeds in them.
   (A) that **(B)** those

Unit 12
Demonstrative Pronouns

Life in the Forest

Which verb correctly completes each sentence?

10. This _____ part of a forest.
(A) are **(B)** is

11. These _____ only some of the forest's animals.
(A) are **(B)** is

12. This _____ a cluster of thick trees.
(A) show **(B)** shows

13. Those _____ trees in which some animals can live.
(A) are **(B)** is

14. That _____ the forest continue its type of life cycle.
(A) help **(B)** helps

15. That _____ to how living things grow, interact, and eventually die.
(A) refer **(B)** refers

16. This _____ me of the way plants and flowers grow.
(A) remind **(B)** reminds

17. Those _____ short life cycles compared to people.
(A) have **(B)** has

18. This _____ a forest similar to where my family and I have camped.
(A) are **(B)** is

19. That _____ seeing deer and rabbits.
(A) include **(B)** includes

20. These _____ important places to learn about nature.
(A) are **(B)** is

The Third LAP
Language Activity Pages

A. Exercising Your Skill

You have been learning about double negatives, indefinite pronouns, and demonstrative pronouns. Number your paper from 1 to 6. Read the sentences below. Use a word from the box only once to complete each sentence correctly.

singular	negative	demonstrative
affirmative	indefinite	double

1. A _____ word expresses the idea of "no."
2. An _____ word expresses the idea of "yes."
3. Two negative words that express the same idea form a _____ negative.
4. An _____ pronoun refers to a person, a place, or a thing that is not specific.
5. When the pronoun *each* is the subject of a sentence, the verb is always _____.
6. A _____ pronoun refers to a person, a place, or a thing that is specific.

B. Expanding Your Skill

Number your paper from 1 to 12. Read the sentences below. For each underlined word, write **N** if it is negative or **A** if it is affirmative.

1. Our store hardly stocks that item.
2. Nowhere in this state can I find it.
3. Have you called any stores out of state?
4. Some place has to have it.
5. If you find the item, then somebody can mail it to you.
6. Nobody could refuse after you had searched so long for it.
7. If anything, you may have to pay a shipping and handling fee.
8. I have scarcely heard of such difficulty trying to find an item.
9. I will try to stock all of that brand's items someday.
10. Everyone should be able to get the products they need.
11. I never want a customer of mine to go through this again.
12. Nothing should be this much of a hassle.

C. Exploring Language

Narrative Writing Number your paper from 1 to 10. Read the story below. If the underlined indefinite pronoun is singular, write the letter **S** on your paper. If it is plural, write the letter **P** on your paper.

Memories of Michigan

Everybody from my dad's family lives in Ohio. Everyone on my mom's side of the family lives in Michigan. Since we live in Ohio, many of our vacations are spent in different parts of Michigan. Much is available to do in Michigan. There are outdoor and indoor types of activities; both can be fun and educational. Several of our vacations were spent boating, skiing, hiking, and cycling. Others were spent at museums, plays, festivals, sporting events, and colleges. Few of our family trips combine both types of activities because of when we go or where we go in Michigan. Each of my family members looks forward to a new adventure when we visit Michigan. Nobody has any complaints yet!

D. Expressing Yourself

Choose one of these activities. When you are finished, give your paper to your teacher.

1. Select two things in the classroom. One thing should refer to the singular, such as a book or a puzzle. The other should refer to the plural, such as the book's pages or the puzzle's pieces. Create two columns on your paper. Leave space at the top of the columns for each thing's name. Write a list of three clues to describe each thing using demonstrative pronouns correctly, such as *This has four sides* or *These are part of a whole.* Ask your teacher to read the clues to guess what each thing is, and write the answers at the top of each column.

2. WORK with a PARTNER Find a partner. Both of you should select one thing in the classroom. Without letting your partner see your paper, write a list of five clues to describe the thing you chose, using demonstrative pronouns correctly. If the thing you chose is singular, use *this* or *that.* If the thing you chose is plural, use *these* or *those.* Remember to decide if the thing is nearby or at a distance. Switch papers, and read your partner's clues. Write the name of what you think your partner described, and switch papers again to check your answers.

Unit 13
Problem Verbs

In speaking and writing, some verb forms are commonly confused and then used incorrectly: *went/gone, saw/seen, did/done,* and *ran/run.*

- *Went, saw, did,* and *ran* are past-tense verb forms and do not need helping verbs.

  Charlotte **went** to the movies. She **saw** her favorite movie.
  Charlotte **did** her chores before she left. She **ran** to the movies.

- *Gone, seen, done,* and *run* are past participles and require helping verbs, including *have, has,* and *had.*

  Martin had **gone** to the park. He had **seen** a friend from school.
  Martin had **done** his homework. He had **run** to the park.

An Attic Surprise

Which verb correctly completes each sentence?

1. One rainy day, my brother and I _____ into our attic.
   (A) went **(B)** gone

2. We had _____ into our attic several times.
   (A) went **(B)** gone

3. On this day, we _____ something we had not noticed before.
   (A) saw **(B)** seen

4. We _____ not want to open it without asking our parents.
   (A) did **(B)** done

5. Once downstairs, I _____ to find our parents.
   (A) ran **(B)** run

6. They had _____ some cleaning in the attic earlier that week.
   (A) did **(B)** done

7. I had _____ by the kitchen and found our parents there.
   (A) ran **(B)** run

8. I _____ into the kitchen, and they said to open what we found.
   (A) went **(B)** gone

Unit 13
Problem Verbs

9. We had _____ an old storage trunk.
(A) saw (B) seen

10. Stuff our parents wanted to keep had _____ into this trunk.
(A) went (B) gone

11. After we opened the trunk, my brother and I _____ familiar items.
(A) saw (B) seen

12. I found awards for races I had _____.
(A) ran (B) run

13. My brother found drawings he had _____ at school.
(A) did (B) done

14. We _____ many photographs of both of us as babies.
(A) saw (B) seen

15. There were other photographs I had never _____.
(A) saw (B) seen

16. I _____ find one of my favorite photographs.
(A) did (B) done

17. It was from when we all _____ to the beach.
(A) went (B) gone

18. Though I disliked the sand, I _____ like the sound of the waves.
(A) did (B) done

19. If we had not _____ the trunk, I would not have the photograph.
(A) saw (B) seen

20. I am glad we _____ into the attic on that rainy day.
(A) went (B) gone

Unit 14
Problem Verbs

Some verb meanings are commonly confused and then used incorrectly, such as *leave/let, lie/lay,* and *set/sit.*

- Do *not* use *leave* in place of *let. Leave* means "to go away," and *let* means "to allow."
  Incorrect: **Let** me alone to read. Correct: **Leave** me alone to read.
  Incorrect: Please **leave** me do that. Correct: Please **let** me do that.
- Do *not* confuse *lie* with *lay. Lie* means "to rest or recline," and *lay* means "to place or put." *Lay* is followed by an object, but *lie* is not.
  Incorrect: **Lay** down on your towel. Correct: **Lie** down on your towel.
  Incorrect: **Lie** the newspaper here. Correct: **Lay** the newspaper here.
- Do *not* use *set* in place of *sit. Set* means "to place or put," and *sit* means "to be seated." *Set* is usually followed by an object, but *sit* is not.
  Incorrect: **Set** by me at dinner. Correct: **Sit** by me at dinner.
  Incorrect: **Sit** the tests on my desk. Correct: **Set** the tests on my desk.

Which verb correctly completes each sentence?

1. Many patients need to _____ still.
   (A) lay **(B)** lie

2. I taught my dog how to _____, stay, and fetch.
   (A) sit **(B)** set

3. Please _____ me help you carry your luggage.
   (A) leave **(B)** let

4. _____ the presents on the table.
   (A) Sit **(B)** Set

5. You should _____ your coat on that chair.
   (A) lay **(B)** lie

6. _____ down if you feel dizzy.
   (A) Lay **(B)** Lie

7. When did he _____ work?
   (A) leave **(B)** let

8. The principal will _____ no earlier than 5:30 P.M.
(A) leave **(B)** let

9. Would you like to _____ next to Lynette?
(A) sit **(B)** set

10. _____ John show you his new skates.
(A) Leave **(B)** Let

11. I saw Irene and June _____ for practice.
(A) leave **(B)** let

12. Please _____ the dishes gently on this shelf.
(A) sit **(B)** set

13. _____ the blanket where I can find it.
(A) Lay **(B)** Lie

14. Did you _____ Pam borrow your volleyball?
(A) leave **(B)** let

15. They _____ their money on the store's counter.
(A) sit **(B)** set

16. Byron likes to _____ on the beach after he swims.
(A) lay **(B)** lie

17. If the weather is mild tomorrow, let's _____ outside for lunch.
(A) sit **(B)** set

18. We _____ the tent outside to dry.
(A) sit **(B)** set

19. Should you _____ the materials there for the next class?
(A) lay **(B)** lie

Unit 14
Problem Verbs

Other confused verb meanings include *go/say, raise/rise,* and *can/may.*

- Do *not* use *go* in place of *say. Go* means "to move along," and *say* means "to speak."

  Incorrect: I **go**, "How is Bradley?"   Correct: I **say**, "How is Bradley?"

- Do *not* confuse *raise* with *rise. Raise* means "to move to a higher point," and *rise* means "to stand or get up." *Raise* is usually followed by an object, but *rise* is not.

  Incorrect: Did she **rise** her hand?   Correct: Did she **raise** her hand?

  Incorrect: I **raise** from my chair.   Correct: I **rise** from my chair.

- Do *not* confuse *can* with *may. Can* refers to ability and means "to know how." *May* expresses possibility and means "to ask permission." *Can* expresses certainty, but *may* does not.

  Incorrect: I **may** use this tool.   Correct: I **can** use this tool.

  Incorrect: **Can** we visit soon?   Correct: **May** we visit soon?

Which verb correctly completes each sentence?

20. _____ the curtain so the audience can see the actors.
(A) Raise **(B)** Rise

21. What did she _____ to the customer?
(A) go **(B)** say

22. This pilot _____ fly most airplanes.
(A) can **(B)** may

23. Please _____ as the judge enters the courtroom.
(A) raise **(B)** rise

24. How do you _____ "hello" in Chinese?
(A) go **(B)** say

25. These questions _____ be on the quiz tomorrow.
(A) can **(B)** may

26. The tape measure does not _____ that far.
(A) go **(B)** say

Unit 14
Problem Verbs

27. The orchestra members _____ from their seats.
(A) raise **(B)** rise

28. The general will _____ the flag at halftime.
(A) raise **(B)** rise

29. I _____ play the violin very well.
(A) can **(B)** may

30. During the fire drill, _____ calmly and exit the building.
(A) raise **(B)** rise

31. Shall we all _____ in the same car?
(A) go **(B)** say

32. _____ Alana and I go to the library after school?
(A) Can **(B)** May

33. Kyle will _____ whether or not they got lost.
(A) go **(B)** say

34. _____ your arms as you stretch.
(A) Raise **(B)** Rise

35. The architect _____ design several styles of homes.
(A) can **(B)** may

36. I will _____ my hand and wave if I see you.
(A) raise **(B)** rise

37. The moon seemed to _____ right out of the cloud.
(A) raise **(B)** rise

38. Did your father _____ to the same college?
(A) go **(B)** say

Unit 15
Misused Words

With so many rules, it is easy to understand how words are misused.

- *A* and *an* are **articles** that describe one of a group. Listen to a word's beginning sound to know which article to use. Do *not* confuse a word's beginning sound with its spelling. Use *a* before words that begin with consonant sounds and *an* before words that begin with vowel sounds.

  Incorrect: **a** hour **an** union Correct: **an** hour **a** union

- *Good* is an adjective used before nouns, and after linking verbs to describe a sentence's subject. *Well* can be an adverb to describe action verbs.

  Good teams work hard. The team looks **good** in their uniforms.
  Incorrect: Did they play **good**? Correct: Did they play **well**?

- *Fewer* and *less* are adjectives. Use *fewer* to describe nouns that can be counted. Use *less* to describe nouns that cannot be counted.

  There are **fewer** players on the field than on the sidelines.
  Those players have **less** dirt on their uniforms.

Hospitals

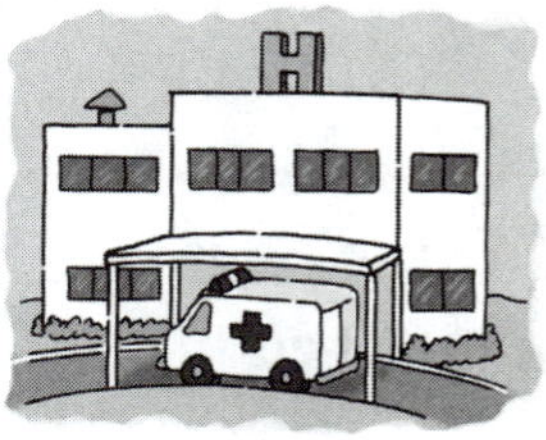

Which word correctly completes each sentence?

1. A hospital can be _____ enormous place.
   (A) a **(B)** an

2. A _____ hospital has many specialists available to its patients.
   (A) good **(B)** well

3. In an emergency, _____ doctor in the emergency room can help.
   (A) a **(B)** an

4. Some emergency rooms have _____ doctors on staff than others.
   (A) fewer **(B)** less

5. With few patients, _____ time should be spent waiting for a doctor.
   (A) fewer **(B)** less

6. No matter where you are in a hospital, you should be treated _____.
   (A) good **(B)** well

Unit 15

Misused Words

It's Fun to Write

7. Our teacher gave us _____ assignment.
(A) a **(B)** an

8. He told us to write _____ essay about our best vacation ever.
(A) a **(B)** an

9. He said it would be a _____ idea to include a photo or a drawing.
(A) good **(B)** well

10. I had _____ question about the assignment.
(A) a **(B)** an

11. I asked, "Could we interview people if we do it _____?"
(A) good **(B)** well

12. He said it is okay if the interviewers ask _____ than ten questions.
(A) fewer **(B)** less

13. Our teacher gave us a _____ amount of time to start our essays.
(A) good **(B)** well

14. I made _____ list of ideas, chose one idea, and began my essay.
(A) a **(B)** an

15. I wrote about a family vacation to Arizona that went very _____.
(A) good **(B)** well

16. I had _____ trouble with this assignment than I thought I would.
(A) fewer **(B)** less

Unit 15
Misused Words

More examples of words that are incorrectly used in place of one another include *among/between, beside/besides,* and *than/then.*

- *Among* shows a relationship with more than two persons or things. In general, *between* shows a relationship with two persons or things.
  There was excitement **among** the students.
  They chose **between** free class time or less homework.
- *Beside* means "at or by the side of," and *besides* means "also; in addition to."
  Jill sat **beside** Max. **Besides** math, they studied social studies.
- *Than* is used to introduce the second part of a comparison. It can connect ideas that are linked. *Then* is an adverb that means "at that time." It helps to express when something happened.
  I am taller **than** Theo in this photo. We were third graders **then**.

A Summer Carnival

Which word correctly completes each sentence?

17. _____ the people in line, we waited to ride the Ferris wheel.
(A) Among **(B)** Between

18. I stood _____ my mom and dad.
(A) among **(B)** between

19. The Ferris wheel's operator waited _____ the ride.
(A) beside **(B)** besides

20. We have been more excited for this ride _____ any other.
(A) than **(B)** then

21. _____ the Ferris wheel, we have waited to ride on the carousel.
(A) Beside **(B)** Besides

22. It was before _____ that we ate our favorite carnival snacks.
(A) than **(B)** then

Unit 15
Misused Words

Go Team, Go!

23. Students from our school sat _____ the home team crowd.
(A) among **(B)** between

24. Alonzo arrived later _____ he thought he would.
(A) than **(B)** then

25. _____ losing his ticket, Alonzo thought the game started later.
(A) Beside **(B)** Besides

26. I waved to Alonzo, and he walked up the bleachers to sit _____ me.
(A) beside **(B)** besides

27. _____ the third and fourth quarters, we bought something to drink.
(A) Among **(B)** Between

28. I would have drunk water at halftime, but I was not thirsty _____.
(A) than **(B)** then

29. Our team played much better in the fourth quarter _____ the third.
(A) than **(B)** then

30. Alonzo and I cheered loudly _____ all the other fans.
(A) among **(B)** between

31. One player's parents sat _____ us, and they worried about the score.
(A) beside **(B)** besides

32. _____ our team made the winning shot, and we jumped up to cheer.
(A) Than **(B)** Then

Unit 15
Misused Words

Other words that are often confused in speaking and writing include *past/passed, real/really,* and *accept/except.*

- *Past* can be an adjective, a preposition, an adverb, or a noun.

  Adjective: The **past** weekend was relaxing.

  Preposition: On a path, we rode our bicycles **past** many farms.

  Adverb: Which farms did you ride **past**?

  Noun: Many of the barns we saw were from the **past**.

  Passed is the past tense and the past participle of the verb *pass.*

  We **passed** only three cars on the way home.

- *Real* is an adjective used before nouns and after linking verbs to describe a sentence's subject. *Really* is an adverb that describes action verbs, adjectives, and other adverbs.

  The **real** challenge is biking that long. Biking is **really** tiring.

- *Accept* is a verb that means "to agree to; to receive." *Except* can be a preposition that means "but; with the exclusion of."

  I **accept** your offer to go biking. Everyone **except** Lily can go.

Which word correctly completes each sentence?

33. The manager of the restaurant will _____ your application.
(A) accept **(B)** except

34. All employees _____ for those on second shift report here.
(A) accept **(B)** except

35. The _____ manager gave us our paychecks.
(A) past **(B)** passed

36. She _____ them out on Wednesday afternoons.
(A) past **(B)** passed

37. Sometimes our work is _____ exhausting.
(A) real **(B)** really

38. The _____ surprise is that we work on Sundays.
(A) real **(B)** really

Unit 15
Misused Words

39. My dad gathered some photographs from his _____.
(A) past **(B)** passed

40. They were from his childhood, and he was _____ young.
(A) real **(B)** really

41. His hair was reddish, and he had _____ freckles all over his face.
(A) real **(B)** really

42. Time _____ quickly as we looked at the photos.
(A) past **(B)** passed

43. We framed the photos _____ for those that were too small.
(A) accept **(B)** except

44. I was _____ sneaky and hid the photo I liked the best.
(A) real **(B)** really

45. I was not sure, but I hoped my mom would _____ it as a gift.
(A) accept **(B)** except

46. I took the photo to a _____ photographer to have it enlarged.
(A) real **(B)** really

47. I made a frame that looks like one I had _____ recently in a store.
(A) past **(B)** passed

48. All of the frames were on sale _____ for the one I wanted.
(A) accept **(B)** except

49. Photographs are a _____ helpful way to study what has happened.
(A) real **(B)** really

50. I enjoy learning about the _____ because I can compare it to the present.
(A) past **(B)** passed

The Last LAP
Language Activity Pages

A. Exercising Your Skill

You have been learning about words that are commonly confused in speaking and writing, such as particular verb tenses and verb meanings. You have also been learning about a variety of other words that are misused. Number your paper from 1 to 8. Read each sentence below to decide if it is true or false. If it is true, write **T** on your paper. If it is false, write **F.**

1. *Went, saw, did,* and *ran* are past participles.
2. A past participle requires a helping verb.
3. *Leave* means "to go away" and *let* means "to allow."
4. The verbs *lay* and *set* have the same meaning.
5. *Rise* is usually followed by an object, but *raise* is not.
6. *A* and *an* are special adjectives known as articles.
7. The word *real* is an adverb.
8. The word *past* is only an adjective.

B. Expanding Your Skill

Number your paper from 1 to 12. Read the sentences below. If the underlined word is used correctly, write the letter **C** on your paper. If the word is used incorrectly, write the letter **I** on your paper.

1. I had did all of my homework before we left.
2. There was a movie I had seen but would like to see again.
3. I saw the newspaper and looked for movie times.
4. My parents said they would leave me go to the 5:05 P.M. show.
5. All I had to do was sit the table before my friends and I left.
6. My parents would set my dinner in the refrigerator for later.
7. I had an banana and some crackers for a snack before the movie.
8. Fewer people were at the movie this time.
9. My friends and I sat among the ninth and tenth rows.
10. The movie was even better than I remember.
11. Beside the animals in the movie, the music was great.
12. I would gladly accept another invitation to this movie.

C. Exploring Language

Persuasive Writing Number your paper from 1 to 10. Read the paragraph below. Some sentences have two words to choose between. Select and write the word that will complete each sentence correctly.

I like roller skates better than/then in-line skates. In the past/passed, I have tried both. I like roller skates because of where the wheels are located. I can/may balance better on roller skates. Among/Between roller skates and in-line skates, I think roller skates are more comfortable. Most materials used on roller skates are soft, unlike hard roller blade materials. I skate good/well on roller skates. I have fallen fewer/less times on roller skates. If it were not for roller skates, we can/may not have had in-line skates. Both in-line skates and skates look good/well, but I prefer skate laces to blade latches. I have saw/seen more people wearing in-line skates than roller skates. I go/say, "That is great because there will be more roller skates for me!"

D. Expressing Yourself

Choose one of these activities. When you are finished, give your paper to your teacher.

1. Find a picture in a magazine, or look for an actual item in your classroom to describe. As you make your choice, think about these verbs: *leave, let, lie, lay, raise, rise, set,* and *sit.* Your description should include four sentences using four of the listed verbs correctly. If you cannot think of a way to use any of these verbs in your description, write directions about how to do a household task.

2. WORK with a PARTNER Find a partner. Divide the following list of words between you: *a, an, among, between, than, then, real,* and *really.* Each of you should write the four words you have on a sheet of paper. Without letting your partner see your paper, write each of your words in a sentence, but use each word incorrectly. After both of you have finished writing four sentences, switch papers. Now write your partner's sentences correctly. Together, compare the mistakes and what each of you did to correct them.

USAGE Scope and Sequence • *Specific Skill Series for Language Arts*

Unit/Level	Level A	Level B	Level C	Level D	Level E	Level F	Level G	Level H
Unit 1	Subject-Verb Agreement	Subject-Verb Agreement	Subject-Verb Agreement	Subject-Verb Agreement	Subject-Verb Agreement	Subject-Verb Agreement	Subject-Verb Agreement	Subject-Verb Agreement
Unit 2	Subject-Verb Agreement	Subject-Verb Agreement	The Verbs *Be* and *Have*	Subject-Verb Agreement	Subject-Verb Agreement	Subject-Verb Agreement	Subject-Verb Agreement	Subject-Verb Agreement
Unit 3	Subject-Verb Agreement	Subject-Verb Agreement	Subject-Verb Agreement	Adjective-Noun Agreement	Past-Tense Verbs	Subject-Verb Agreement	Past-Tense Verbs	Verb Tenses
Unit 4	Subject-Verb Agreement	Subject-Verb Agreement	Subject-Verb Agreement	Speaking of Yourself Last	Past-Tense Verbs	Past-Tense Verbs	Future Tense	Progressive Forms
Unit 5	The Verb *Be*	Subject-Verb Agreement	Subject-Verb Agreement	Past-Tense Verbs	Past Tense of *Be*	Future Tense	Perfect Tenses	Comparing with Adjectives and Adverbs
Unit 6	The Verb *Have*	The Verb *Be*	Adjective-Noun Agreement	Past Tense of *Be*	Future Tense	Perfect Tenses	Comparing with Adjectives and Adverbs	Participles as Adjectives
Unit 7	Using *This, That, These,* and *Those*	The Verb *Have*	Speaking of Yourself Last	Comparing with Adjectives and Adverbs	Perfect Tenses	Comparing with Adjectives and Adverbs	Participles as Adjectives	Double Negatives
Unit 8	Past-Tense Verbs	Using *This, That, These,* and *Those*	Past-Tense Verbs	Future-Tense Verbs	Comparing with Adjectives and Adverbs	Participles as Adjectives	Double Negatives	Pronouns
Unit 9	Past Tense of *Be*	Adjective-Noun Agreement	Past Tense of *Be*	Perfect-Tense Verbs	Participles as Adjectives	Double Negatives	Pronouns	Avoiding Double Subjects
Unit 10	Comparing with Adjectives	Past-Tense Verbs	Comparing with Adjectives	Perfect-Tense Verbs	Double Negatives	Indefinite Pronouns	Active and Passive Voice	Active and Passive Voice
Unit 11	*A* and *An*	Past Tense of *Be*	Comparing with Adverbs	Verb Tenses	Indefinite Pronouns	Demonstrative Pronouns	Problem Verbs	Keeping Tenses Consistent
Unit 12	Agreement with Helping Verbs	Comparing with Adjectives	*A* and *An*	Double Negatives	Demonstrative Pronouns	Interrogative Pronouns	Misused Words	Problem Verbs
Unit 13		*A* and *An*	Agreement with Helping Verbs	Problem Verbs	Problem Verbs	Active and Passive Voice	Misused Phrases	Misused Words
Unit 14		Agreement with Helping Verbs	Future-Tense Verbs	Misused Words	Problem Verbs	Problem Verbs		Misused Phrases
Unit 15		Agreement with Helping Verbs	Present Perfect Tense		Misused Words	Misused Words		
Unit 16		Future-Tense Verbs	Verb Tenses			Misused Words		
Unit 17		Contractions	Contractions			Misused Phrases		
Unit 18			Double Negatives					
Unit 19			Problem Verbs					